Basketball

by Danton Stone

Content Consultant
Thomas Sawyer, EdD
Professor of Recreation and Sports Management
Indiana State University
Terre Haute, Indiana

Reading Consultant
Jeanne Clidas
Reading Specialist

Children's Press®
An Imprint of Scholastic Inc.
New York Toronto London Auckland · Sydney
Mexico City New Delhi Hong Kong
Danbury, Connecticut

Library of Congress Cataloging-in-Publication Data
Stone, Danton.
  Basketball/by Danton Stone.
    p. cm.—(Rookie read about sports)
  Includes bibliographical references and index.
  ISBN-13: 978-0-531-20866-3 (lib. bdg.)   ISBN-10: 0-531-20866-4 (lib. bdg.)
  ISBN-13: 978-0-531-20935-6 (pbk.)   ISBN-10: 0-531-20935-0 (pbk.)
  1. Basketball—Juvenile literature. I. Title.
  GV885.1.S76 2012
  796.323—dc23   2011037089

1 2 3 4 5 6 7 8 9 10 R 21 20 19 18 17 16 15 14 13 12

Photographs © 2012: Alamy Images/Erik Isakson/Rubberball: 20 bottom; Dreamstime/
Innovatedcaptures: 14; iStockphoto: 12 (CEFutcher), 8, 24 top left, 31 bottom left
(Lawrence Sawyer); Media Bakery: 26 (Deborah Jaffe/Fancy Collection/Corbis),
cover, 18, 22; Shutterstock, Inc.: basketball throughout (Andresr), 16 bottom,
24 bottom left (GeoM), 4 (L. Watcharapol), 10, 24 top right, 31 bottom right
(Mark Stout Photography), 6, 16 top, 20 top, 24 bottom right, 28, 31 top
right (Morgan).

Table of Contents

What Is Basketball?

Basketball is a fun game. Two teams play with a round ball. It is a basketball. The teams play on an indoor or outdoor court.

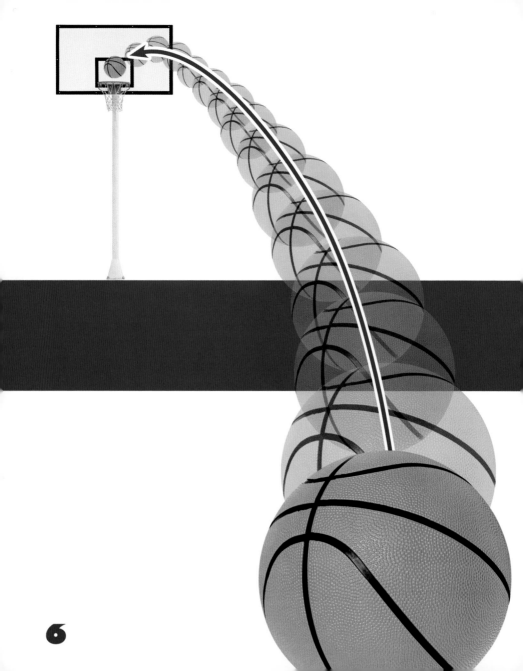

Each team tries to throw the basketball into the basket. First, you must get close to your basket.

Dribble and Pass

How do you get the ball close
to your basket? You can do
this by bouncing the ball.
That is called dribbling.

Passing is another way to move the ball closer to your basket. First, hold the ball. Now pass it to a teammate.

The team passes the ball to each other. The ball moves closer to the basket.

14

Foul!

The official blows his whistle.
Someone broke a rule. You
are not allowed to push or
hold onto another player.
That is called a foul.

Shoot and Score

See the basket? That's
your target. One of you
throws the ball at the basket.
That is called taking a shot.

You can jump in the air to take a shot. That is called a jump shot.

If you miss the shot, catch the ball. That is called getting a rebound.

Get close to the basket again. Shoot the basketball into the basket. Score!

Have Fun!

Basketball is fun.

You can dribble the ball.

You can pass the ball.

You can shoot the ball.

You can score points.

That's how you have fun playing basketball.

Good Sportsmanship

- Respect yourself, the other players, and the adults helping out.
- Always play fair.
- Stay positive. Cheer for your teammates. Learn from your mistakes. And keep playing!
- Be nice to all the players, whether you win or lose.

For . . .

Staying Fit

🏀 Eat right.

- Choose lots of fruits and vegetables.
- Eat 5 servings of grains. Whole wheat bread is good. So is oatmeal.
- Protein keeps you strong. Meat, eggs, and fish give you protein.
- Dairy makes strong bones. Milk and cheese are dairy.

🏀 Get plenty of sleep.

🏀 Play your sport as much as you can. Basketball players need to be strong to throw the ball. They need to run fast on the court. And they need to practice to get their hands and feet to work together when they dribble.

Basketball Fun Facts

- The first baskets were wooden peach baskets.

- Orange basketballs were first used in the 1950s.

Visit this Scholastic web site for more information on basketball:
www.factsfornow.scholastic.com

Words You Know

basket

basketball

dribbling

passing

Index

About the Author

Danton Stone is proud to have acted on Broadway, in London, in films, and on television. He's written plays and taught acting at Columbia University. He is most proud to have taught his daughter to be a fine playground basketball player.